KNIT ACCESSORIES

M000252053

36

LEISURE ARTS, INC. • Maumelle, Arkansas

Looking to try a new knitting technique? Try knitting it in the round! Working in the round is the perfect way to try new knitting skills – you're always looking at the right side of your work, so there's less confusion when you set it down and pick it back up again. Knit Accessories contains seven matching sets, for a total of 14 patterns, which will get you started on knitting cables, textured patterns, lace, and slipped stitches in the round. Grab your yarn and needles and try something fun and new and knit an accessory or two!

22

DREAMY
CABLED BOOT
CUFFS & MITTENS

■■■□ INTERMEDIATE

SHOPPING LIST

Yarn (Bulky Weight) 🧶5

[8.8 ounces, 466 yards
(250 grams, 426 meters) per skein]:

☐ 1 skein

Knitting Needles

Double-pointed (set of 5),

☐ Size 9 (5.5 mm)

or size needed for gauge

Additional Supplies

☐ Split-ring marker

☐ Stitch marker

☐ Stitch holder

☐ Yarn needle

SIZE INFORMATION

BOOT CUFFS

Stretches to fit leg circumferences up to
15{17½-20}"/38{44.5-51} cm

Finished Height: 6" (15 cm)

MITTENS

Fits hand circumference of 7½{9}"/19{23} cm

Finished Length: 9½" (24 cm)

Size Note: We have printed the instructions for
the sizes in different colors to make it easier for
you to find:

• size Small in Blue

• size Medium in Pink

• size Large in Green

Instructions in Black apply to all sizes.

GAUGE INFORMATION

In pattern,

   2 repeats (14 sts) = 3¾" (9.5 cm);

   16 rnds = 2¾" (7 cm)

TECHNIQUES USED

- K2 tog *(Fig. 4, page 44)*
- M1 *(Figs. 7a & b, page 45)*

LEFT TWIST *(abbreviated LT)* (uses next 2 sts)

Working **behind** first stitch on left needle, knit into the **back** of second stitch *(Fig. A)* making sure not to drop stitches off, then knit the first stitch *(Fig. B)* letting both stitches drop off the left needle.

Fig. A

Fig. B

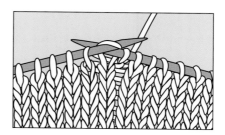

BOOT CUFF (Make 2)

With double-pointed needles, cast on 49{56-63} sts **loosely**.

Divide sts onto 4 needles *(see Using Double-Pointed Needles, page 43)*; place a split-ring marker around the first stitch to indicate the beginning of the round *(see Markers, page 42)*.

Rnd 1 (Right side): ★ P2, K5; repeat from ★ around.

Rnd 2: ★ P2, LT, K3; repeat from ★ around.

Rnd 3: ★ P2, K5; repeat from ★ around.

Rnd 4: ★ P2, K1, LT, K2; repeat from ★ around.

Rnd 5: ★ P2, K5; repeat from ★ around.

Rnd 6: ★ P2, K2, LT, K1; repeat from ★ around.

Rnd 7: ★ P2, K5; repeat from ★ around.

Rnd 8: ★ P2, K3, LT; repeat from ★ around.

Rnd 9: ★ P2, K5; repeat from ★ around.

Rnds 10-33: Repeat Rnds 2-9, 3 times.

Bind off all sts **loosely** in pattern.

MITTEN (Make 2)

Cuff

With double-pointed needles, cast on 28{35} sts.

Divide sts onto 4 needles; place a split-ring marker around the first stitch to indicate the beginning of the round.

Rnd 1 (Right side): ★ P2, K5; repeat from ★ around.

Rnd 2: ★ P2, LT, K3; repeat from ★ around.

Rnd 3: ★ P2, K5; repeat from ★ around.

Rnd 4: ★ P2, K1, LT, K2; repeat from ★ around.

Rnd 5: ★ P2, K5; repeat from ★ around.

Rnd 6: ★ P2, K2, LT, K1; repeat from ★ around.

Rnd 7: ★ P2, K5; repeat from ★ around.

Rnd 8: ★ P2, K3, LT; repeat from ★ around.

Rnd 9: ★ P2, K5; repeat from ★ around.

Rnds 10-17: Repeat Rnds 2-9.

Body

Rnds 1 and 2: Knit around.

GUSSET

Rnd 1: Knit around, place a marker around the right needle, M1: 29{36} sts.

Rnd 2: Knit around to marker, slip marker, K1.

Rnd 3: Knit around to marker, slip marker, M1, K1, M1: 31{38} sts.

Rnd 4: Knit around to marker, slip marker, K3.

Rnd 5: Knit around to marker, slip marker, M1, K3, M1: 33{40} sts.

Rnd 6: Knit around to marker, slip marker, K5.

Rnd 7: Knit around to marker, slip marker, M1, K5, M1: 35{42} sts.

Rnd 8: Knit around to marker, slip marker, K7.

Rnd 9: Knit around to marker, slip marker, M1, K7, M1: 37{44} sts.

Rnd 10: Knit around to marker, slip marker, K9.

HAND

Rnd 1: Knit around to marker, remove marker, place next 9 sts onto st holder: 28{35} sts.

Knit every round until piece measures approximately 8" (20.5 cm) from cast on edge.

SHAPING

Rnd 1: ★ K5, K2 tog; repeat from ★ around: 24{30} sts.

Rnd 2: Knit around.

Rnd 3: ★ K4, K2 tog; repeat from ★ around: 20{25} sts.

Rnd 4: Knit around.

Rnd 5: ★ K3, K2 tog; repeat from ★ around: 16{20} sts.

Rnd 6: ★ K2, K2 tog; repeat from ★ around: 12{15} sts.

Rnd 7: ★ K1, K2 tog; repeat from ★ around: 8{10} sts.

Rnd 8: K2tog around: 4{5} sts.

Cut yarn leaving an 8" (20.5 cm) length for sewing. Thread yarn needle with end and slip remaining sts onto yarn needle; pull **tightly** to close and secure end.

Thumb

Place sts from st holder onto 2 double-pointed needles as follows: Place 5 sts onto Needle 1 and 4 sts onto Needle 2. With Needle 3, pick up 3 sts in the gap where the thumb meets the hand *(Fig. 9, page 45)*; place a split-ring marker around the first stitch to indicate the beginning of the round: 12 sts.

Redistribute sts to have 4 sts on **each** needle.

Rnds 1-6: Knit around.

Rnd 7: K2 tog around: 6 sts.

Rnd 8: K2 tog around: 3 sts.

Cut yarn leaving an 8" (20.5 cm) length for sewing.
Thread yarn needle with end and slip remaining sts onto yarn needle; pull **tightly** to close and secure end.

CLASSIC LACE

C O W L & H A T

◖◼◼▢ INTERMEDIATE

Yarn (Light Weight) 🧶3

[1.75 ounces, 125 yards
(50 grams, 114 meters) per skein]:

☐ 3{4} skeins

Knitting Needles

Double-pointed (set of 5),
16" (40.5 cm) Circular **and**
24" (61 cm) Circular,

☐ Size 6 (4 mm)
  or size needed for gauge

Additional Supplies

☐ Stitch marker
☐ Split-ring marker
☐ Tapestry needle

SIZE INFORMATION

COWL
Finished Circumference:
22¾{44}"/58{112} cm
Finished Height: 7½" (19 cm)
HAT
Fits head circumference up to
20{23}"/51{58.5} cm
Finished Height: 9½" (24 cm)

Size Note: We have printed the instructions for
the sizes in different colors to make it easier for
you to find:

• size Medium in Pink
• size Large in Green

Instructions in Black apply to both sizes.

GAUGE INFORMATION

In Body pattern,

    2 repeats (16 sts) = 3¼" (8.25 cm);

    32 rnds = 4¼" (10.75 cm)

TECHNIQUES USED

- K2 tog *(Fig. 4, page 44)*
- SSK *(Figs. 5a-c, page 44)*
- YO *(Fig. 8, page 45)*

COWL

Bottom Ribbing

With 24" (61 cm) circular needle, cast on 112{216} sts **loosely** *(see Using Circular Needles, page 43)*; place a marker to indicate the beginning of the round *(see Markers, page 42)*.

Rnds 1-8: ★ K1, P2, K3, P2; repeat from ★ around.

Body

Rnds 1 and 2: Knit around.

Rnd 3: K4, YO, SSK, ★ K6, YO, SSK; repeat from ★ around to last 2 sts, K2.

Rnd 4: Knit around.

Rnd 5: K2, K2 tog, YO, K1, YO, SSK, ★ K3, K2 tog, YO, K1, YO, SSK; repeat from ★ around to last st, K1.

Rnd 6: Knit around.

Rnd 7: K4, YO, SSK, ★ K6, YO, SSK; repeat from ★ around to last 2 sts, K2.

Rnds 8-10: Knit around.

Rnd 11: ★ YO, SSK, K6; repeat from ★ around.

Rnd 12: Knit around.

Rnd 13: ★ K1, YO, SSK, K3, K2 tog, YO; repeat from ★ around.

Rnd 14: Knit around.

Rnd 15: ★ YO, SSK, K6; repeat from ★ around.

Rnds 16-18: Knit around.

Rnds 19-41: Repeat Rnds 3-18 once, then repeat Rnds 3-9 once **more**.

Top Ribbing

Rnds 1-8: ★ K1, P2, K3, P2; repeat from ★ around.

Bind off all sts **loosely** in pattern.

HAT
Ribbing

With 16" (40.5 cm) circular needle, cast on 88{104} sts **loosely**; place a marker to indicate the beginning of the round.

Rnds 1-12: ★ K1, P2, K3, P2; repeat from ★ around.

Body

Rnds 1 and 2: Knit around.

Rnd 3: K4, YO, SSK, ★ K6, YO, SSK; repeat from ★ around to last 2 sts, K2.

Rnd 4: Knit around.

Rnd 5: K2, K2 tog, YO, K1, YO, SSK, ★ K3, K2 tog, YO, K1, YO, SSK; repeat from ★ around to last st, K1.

Rnd 6: Knit around.

Rnd 7: K4, YO, SSK, ★ K6, YO, SSK; repeat from ★ around to last 2 sts, K2.

Rnds 8-10: Knit around.

Rnd 11: ★ YO, SSK, K6; repeat from ★ around.

Rnd 12: Knit around.

Rnd 13: ★ K1, YO, SSK, K3, K2 tog, YO; repeat from ★ around.

Rnd 14: Knit around.

Rnd 15: ★ YO, SSK, K6; repeat from ★ around.

Rnds 16-18: Knit around.

Rnds 19-48: Repeat Rnds 3-18 once, then repeat Rnds 3-16 once **more**.

SHAPING

Change to double-pointed needles when there are too few stitches to use a circular needle *(see Using Double-Pointed Needles, page 43)*.

Rnd 1: ★ K6, K2 tog; repeat from ★ around: 77{91} sts.

Rnds 2 and 3: Knit around.

Rnd 4: ★ K5, K2 tog; repeat from ★ around: 66{78} sts.

Rnds 5 and 6: Knit around.

Rnd 7: ★ K4, K2 tog; repeat from ★ around: 55{65} sts.

Rnd 8: Knit around.

Rnd 9: ★ K3, K2 tog; repeat from ★ around: 44{52} sts.

Rnd 10: Knit around.

Rnd 11: ★ K2, K2 tog; repeat from ★ around: 33{39} sts.

Rnd 12: ★ K1, K2 tog; repeat from ★ around: 22{26} sts.

Rnd 13: K2 tog around: 11{13} sts.

Cut yarn leaving an 8" (20.5 cm) length for sewing.
Thread tapestry needle with end and slip remaining sts onto tapestry needle; pull **tightly** to close and secure end.

16

36

SILKY SATIN

HAT &
FINGERLESS MITTS

■■■□ **INTERMEDIATE**

SHOPPING LIST

Yarn (Medium Weight) 🏷4 MEDIUM

[3.5 ounces, 200 yards
(100 grams, 182 meters) per skein]:

☐ 2 skeins

Knitting Needles

Double-pointed (set of 5) **and**

16" (40.5 cm) Circular,

☐ Size 8 (5 mm)

or size needed for gauge

Additional Supplies

☐ Stitch marker

☐ Split-ring marker

☐ Stitch holder

☐ Yarn needle

SIZE INFORMATION

HAT

Fits head circumference up to

20{23}"/51{58.5} cm

Finished Height: 9½" (24 cm)

MITTENS

Fits hand circumference of 7½{9}"/19{23} cm

Finished Length: 9½" (24 cm)

Size Note: We have printed the instructions for

the sizes in different colors to make it easier for

you to find:

• size Medium in Pink

• size Large in Green

Instructions in Black apply to both sizes.

GAUGE INFORMATION

In Body pattern, 3 repeats (18 sts)
and 32 rnds = 4" (10 cm)

TECHNIQUES USED

- K2 tog *(Fig. 4, page 44)*
- SSK *(Figs. 5a-c, page 44)*
- M1 *(Figs. 7a & b, page 45)*

HAT
Ribbing

With 16" (40.5 cm) circular needle, cast on 84{96} sts **loosely** *(see Using Circular Needles, page 43)*; place a marker to indicate the beginning of the round *(see Markers, page 42)*.

Rnds 1-12: ★ P2, K2; repeat from ★ around.

Body

Rnd 1 (Right side)**:** Knit around.

Rnd 2: K1, P4, ★ K2, P4; repeat from ★ around to last st, K1.

Rnd 3: Knit around.

Rnd 4: P2, K2, ★ P4, K2; repeat from ★ around to last 2 sts, P2.

Repeat Rnds 1-4 for pattern until piece measures approximately 8" (20.5 cm) from cast on edge, ending by working Rnd 4.

SHAPING

Change to double-pointed needles when there are too few stitches to use a circular needle *(see Using Double-Pointed Needles, page 43)*.

Rnd 1: ★ K2 tog, K8, SSK; repeat from ★ around: 70{80} sts.

Rnd 2: K1, P3, ★ K2, P3; repeat from ★ around to last st, K1.

Rnd 3: Knit around.

Rnd 4: ★ K2 tog, K1, P4, K1, SSK; repeat from ★ around: 56{64} sts.

Rnd 5: Knit around.

Rnd 6: K1, P2, ★ K2, P2; repeat from ★ around to last st, K1.

Rnd 7: ★ K2 tog, K4, SSK; repeat from ★ around: 42{48} sts.

Rnd 8: K1, P4, ★ K2, P4; repeat from ★ around to last st, K1.

Rnd 9: ★ K2 tog, K2, SSK; repeat from ★ around: 28{32} sts.

Rnd 10: Knit around.

Rnd 11: ★ K2 tog, SSK; repeat from ★ around: 14{16} sts.

Rnd 12: K2 tog around: 7{8} sts.

Cut yarn leaving an 8" (20.5 cm) length for sewing.
Thread yarn needle with end and slip remaining sts onto yarn needle; pull **tightly** to close and secure end.

FINGERLESS MITT
(Make 2)
Cuff

With double-pointed needles, cast on 36{40} sts **loosely**.

Divide sts evenly onto 4 needles; place a split-ring marker around the first stitch to indicate the beginning of the round.

Rnds 1 thru 10{9}: ★ P2, K2; repeat from ★ around.

Size Large - Rnd 10: Work in K2, P2 ribbing around working M1 twice evenly spaced: 42 sts.

Body

Rnd 1 (Right side)**:** Knit around.

Rnd 2: K1, P4, ★ K2, P4; repeat from ★ around to last st, K1.

Rnd 3: Knit around.

Rnd 4: P2, K2, ★ P4, K2; repeat from ★ around to last 2 sts, P2.

Repeat Rnds 1-4 for pattern until piece measures approximately 5" (12.5 cm) from cast on edge, ending by working Rnd 4.

GUSSET

Rnd 1: Knit around, place a marker around the right needle, M1: 37{43} sts.

Rnd 2: K1, P4, ★ K2, P4; repeat from ★ around to within one st of marker, K1, slip marker, K1.

Rnd 3: Knit around to marker, slip marker, M1, K1, M1: 39{45} sts.

Rnd 4: P2, K2, ★ P4, K2; repeat from ★ around to within 2 sts of marker, P2, slip marker, K3.

Rnd 5: Knit around to marker, slip marker, M1, K3, M1: 41{47} sts.

Rnd 6: K1, P4, ★ K2, P4; repeat from ★ around to within one st of marker, K1, slip marker, K5.

Rnd 7: Knit around to marker, slip marker, M1, K5, M1: 43{49} sts.

Rnd 8: P2, K2, ★ P4, K2; repeat from ★ around to within 2 sts of marker, P2, slip marker, K7.

Rnd 9: Knit around to marker, slip marker, M1, K7, M1: 45{51} sts.

Rnd 10: K1, P4, ★ K2, P4; repeat from ★ around to within one st of marker, K1, slip marker, K9.

HAND

Rnd 1: Knit around to marker, remove marker, place next 9 sts onto st holder: 36{42} sts.

Rnd 2: P2, K2, ★ P4, K2; repeat from ★ around to last 2 sts, P2.

Rnd 3: Knit around.

Rnd 4: K1, P4, ★ K2, P4; repeat from ★ around to last st, K1.

Rnd 5: Knit around.

Rnd 6: P2, K2, ★ P4, K2; repeat from ★ around to last 2 sts, P2.

Ribbing

Rnds 1-6: ★ P2, K2; repeat from ★ around.

Bind off all sts **loosely** in ribbing.

Thumb

Place sts from st holder onto 2 double-pointed needles as follows: Place 5 sts onto Needle 1 and 4 sts onto Needle 2. With Needle 3, pick up 3 sts in the gap where the thumb meets the hand *(Fig. 9, page 45)*; place a split-ring marker around the first stitch to indicate the beginning of the round: 12 sts.

Redistribute sts to have 4 sts on **each** needle.

Rnds 1-3: Knit around.

Rnds 4-7: ★ P2, K2; repeat from ★ around.

Bind off all sts **loosely** in ribbing.

GO TEAM
COWL & HEADBAND
■■□□ EASY +

SHOPPING LIST

Yarn (Super Bulky) 🧶 6 SUPER BULKY

[5 ounces, 81 yards

(142 grams, 74 meters) per skein]:

☐ 2{3} skeins

Knitting Needles

16" (40.5 cm) Circular **and**

24" (61 cm) Circular,

☐ Size 11 (8 mm)

or size needed for gauge

Additional Supplies

☐ Stitch marker

SIZE INFORMATION

COWL

Finished Circumference:

Stretches up to 24{48}"/61{122} cm

Finished Height: 8½" (21.5 cm)

HEADBAND

Fits head circumference up to

20{23}"/51{58.5} cm

Finished Height: 3¾" (9.5 cm)

Size Note: We have printed the instructions for

the sizes in different colors to make it easier

for you to find:

- size Medium in Pink
- size Large in Green

Instructions in Black apply to both sizes.

GAUGE INFORMATION
In pattern (slightly stretched),
2 repeats (10 sts) and
17 rnds = 4" (10 cm)

COWL

With 24" (61 cm) circular needle, cast on 60{120} sts **loosely** *(see Using Circular Needles, page 43)*; place a marker to indicate the beginning of the round *(see Markers, page 42)*.

Rnd 1 (Right side)**:** ★ K3, P2; repeat from ★ around.

Rnd 2: ★ K1, wyif slip 1 as if to **purl**, wyib K1, P2; repeat from ★ around.

Rnds 3-35: Repeat Rnds 1 and 2, 16 times; then repeat Rnd 1 once **more**.

Bind off all sts **loosely** in pattern.

HEADBAND

With 16" (40.5 cm) circular needle, cast on 40{50} sts **loosely**; place a marker to indicate the beginning of the round.

Rnd 1 (Right side)**:** ★ K3, P2; repeat from ★ around.

Rnd 2: ★ K1, wyif slip 1 as if to **purl**, wyib K1, P2; repeat from ★ around.

Rnds 3-15: Repeat Rnds 1 and 2, 6 times; then repeat Rnd 1 once **more**.

Bind off all sts **loosely** in pattern.

EASY CABLED

BOOT CUFFS & HEADBAND

 **INTERMEDIATE**

Yarn (Medium Weight) 🧶 **4**

[3 ounces, 197 yards

(85 grams, 180 meters) per skein]:

☐ 2 skeins

Knitting Needles

Double-pointed (set of 5) **and**

16" (40.5 cm) Circular,

☐ Size 8 (5 mm)

or size needed for gauge

Additional Supplies

☐ Split-ring marker

☐ Stitch marker

☐ Cable needle

BOOT CUFFS

Stretches to fit calf circumferences up to

15{17½-20}"/38{44.5-51} cm

Finished Height: 5¾" (14.5 cm)

HEADBAND

Fits head circumference up to

20{23}"/51{58.5} cm

Finished Height: 3¾" (9.5 cm)

Size Note: We have printed the instructions for

the sizes in different colors to make it easier for

you to find:

• size Small in Blue

• size Medium in Pink

• size Large in Green

Instructions in Black apply to all sizes.

GAUGE INFORMATION

In pattern,
    2 repeats (16 sts) = 3" (7.5 cm);
    32 rnds = 4" (10 cm)

LEFT PURL CROSS *(abbreviated LPC)* (uses next 4 sts)
Slip next 2 sts onto cable needle and hold in **front** of work, P2 from left needle, K2 from cable needle.

RIGHT PURL CROSS *(abbreviated RPC)* (uses next 4 sts)
Slip next 2 sts onto cable needle and hold in **back** of work, K2 from left needle, P2 from cable needle.

BOOT CUFF (Make 2)

With double-pointed needles, cast on 64{72-80} sts **loosely**.

Divide sts evenly onto 4 needles *(see Using Double-Pointed Needles, page 43)*; place a split-ring marker around the first stitch to indicate the beginning of the round *(see Markers, page 42)*.

Rnd 1 (Right side)**:** P2, K4, ★ P4, K4; repeat from ★ around to last 2 sts, P2.

Rnd 2: Knit around.

Rnds 3-6: Repeat Rnds 1 and 2 twice.

Rnd 7: ★ work LPC, work RPC; repeat from ★ around.

Rnd 8: Knit around.

Rnds 9-44: Repeat Rnds 1-8, 4 times; then repeat Rnds 1-4 once **more**.

Bind off all sts **loosely** in pattern.

HEADBAND

With circular needle, cast on 96{104} sts **loosely** *(see Using Circular Needles, page 43)*; place a marker to indicate the beginning of the round.

Rnd 1 (Right side)**:** P2, K4, ★ P4, K4; repeat from ★ around to last 2 sts, P2.

Rnd 2: Knit around.

Rnds 3-6: Repeat Rnds 1 and 2 twice.

Rnd 7: ★ work LPC, work RPC; repeat from ★ around.

Rnd 8: Knit around.

Rnds 9-28: Repeat Rnds 1-8 twice, then repeat Rnds 1-4 once **more**.

Bind off all sts **loosely** in pattern.

WRAPPED IN LOVE

C O W L & M I T T E N S

 **INTERMEDIATE**

Yarn (Medium Weight) **4**

[4.5 ounces, 200 yards

(127 grams, 183 meters) per skein]:

☐ 2{3} skeins

Knitting Needles

Double-pointed (set of 5) **and**

24" (61 cm) Circular,

☐ Size 9 (5.5 mm)

or size needed for gauge

Additional Supplies

☐ Stitch marker

☐ Split-ring marker

☐ Stitch holder

☐ Yarn needle

COWL

Finished Circumference:

25{50}"/63.5{127} cm

Finished Height: 9" (23 cm)

MITTENS

Fits hand circumference of 7½{9}"/19{23} cm

Finished Length: 9" (23 cm)

Size Note: We have printed the instructions

for the sizes in different colors to make it

easier for you to find:

• size Medium in Pink

• size Large in Green

Instructions in Black apply to both sizes.

GAUGE INFORMATION

In pattern, one repeat (10 sts) and
20 rnds = 2½" (6.25 cm)

TECHNIQUES USED

- K2 tog *(Fig. 4, page 44)*
- P2 tog *(Fig. 6, page 44)*
- M1 *(Figs. 7a & b, page 45)*

COWL

With 24" (61 cm) circular needle, cast on 100{200} sts **loosely** *(see Using Circular Needles, page 43)*; place a marker to indicate the beginning of the round *(see Markers, page 42)*.

Rnds 1 and 2: ★ K5, P5; repeat from ★ around.

Rnds 3 and 4: ★ P5, K5; repeat from ★ around.

Rnds 5-70: Repeat Rnds 1-4, 16 times; then repeat Rnds 1 and 2 once **more**.

Bind off all sts **loosely** in pattern.

MITTEN (Make 2)
Body

With double-pointed needles, cast on 30{40} sts **loosely**.

Divide sts onto 4 needles *(see Using Double-Pointed Needles, page 43)*; place a split-ring marker around the first stitch to indicate the beginning of the round.

Rnds 1 and 2: ★ K5, P5; repeat from ★ around.

Rnds 3 and 4: ★ P5, K5; repeat from ★ around.

Rnds 5-25: Repeat Rnds 1-4, 5 times; then repeat Rnd 1 once **more**.

GUSSET
Rnd 1: ★ K5, P5; repeat from ★ around, place a marker around the right needle, M1: 31{41} sts.

Rnd 2: ★ P5, K5; repeat from ★ around to marker, slip marker, K1.

Rnd 3: ★ P5, K5; repeat from ★ around to marker, slip marker, M1, K1, M1: 33{43} sts.

Rnd 4: ★ K5, P5; repeat from ★ around to marker, slip marker, K3.

Rnd 5: ★ K5, P5; repeat from ★ around to marker, slip marker, M1, K3, M1: 35{45} sts.

Rnd 6: ★ P5, K5; repeat from ★ around to marker, slip marker, K5.

Rnd 7: ★ P5, K5; repeat from ★ around to marker, slip marker, M1, K5, M1: 37{47} sts.

Rnd 8: ★ K5, P5; repeat from ★ around to marker, slip marker, K7.

Rnd 9: ★ K5, P5; repeat from ★ around to marker, slip marker, M1, K7, M1: 39{49} sts.

Rnd 10: ★ P5, K5; repeat from ★ around to marker, slip marker, K9.

HAND

Rnd 1: ★ P5, K5; repeat from ★ around to marker, remove marker, place next 9 sts onto st holder: 30{40} sts.

Rnds 2 and 3: ★ K5, P5; repeat from ★ around.

Rnds 4 and 5: ★ P5, K5; repeat from ★ around.

Rnds 6-27: Repeat Rnds 2-5, 5 times; then repeat Rnds 2 and 3 once **more**.

SHAPING

Rnd 1: ★ P2 tog, P3, K5; repeat from ★ around: 27{36} sts.

Rnd 2: ★ P4, K5; repeat from ★ around.

Rnd 3: ★ K2 tog, K2, P5; repeat from ★ around: 24{32} sts.

Rnd 4: ★ K3, P5; repeat from ★ around.

Rnd 5: ★ P2 tog, P1, K5; repeat from ★ around: 21{28} sts.

Rnd 6: ★ P2 tog, K5; repeat from ★ around: 18{24} sts.

Rnd 7: ★ P2 tog, P4; repeat from ★ around: 15{20} sts.

Rnd 8: ★ P2 tog, P3; repeat from ★ around: 12{16} sts.

Rnd 9: ★ K2 tog, K2; repeat from ★ around: 9{12} sts.

Rnd 10: ★ K2 tog, K1; repeat from ★ around: 6{8} sts.

Cut yarn leaving an 8" (20.5 cm) length for sewing.
Thread yarn needle with end and slip remaining sts onto yarn needle; pull **tightly** to close and secure end.

Thumb

Place sts from st holder onto 2 double-pointed needles as follows: Place 5 sts onto Needle 1 and 4 sts onto Needle 2. With Needle 3, pick up 3 sts in the gap where the thumb meets the hand *(Fig. 9, page 45)*; place a split-ring marker around the first stitch to indicate the beginning of the round: 12 sts.

Redistribute sts to have 4 sts on **each** needle.

Rnds 1-8: Knit around.

Rnd 9: K2 tog around: 6 sts.

Rnd 10: K2 tog around: 3 sts.

Cut yarn leaving an 8" (20.5 cm) length for sewing.
Thread yarn needle with end and slip remaining sts onto yarn needle; pull **tightly** to close and secure end.

16

4

CHUNKY

SLIPPED STITCH COWL & HAT

 **INTERMEDIATE**

Yarn (Bulky Weight) **5**

[3.5 ounces, 148 yards
(100 grams, 136 meters) per skein]:

☐ MC (Pink) - 2 skeins

☐ CC (Off White) - 1 skein

Knitting Needles

Double-pointed (set of 5),
16" (40.5 cm) Circular **and**
24" (61 cm) Circular,

☐ Size 10 (6 mm)

or size needed for gauge

Additional Supplies

☐ Stitch marker

☐ Split-ring marker

☐ Yarn needle

COWL

Finished Circumference:
29¾{59½}"/75.5{151} cm

Finished Height: 5½" (14 cm)

HAT

Fits head circumference up to
20{23}"/51{58.5} cm

Finished Height: 9¼" (23.5 cm)

Size Note: We have printed the instructions for
the sizes in different colors to make it easier for
you to find:

· size Medium in Pink

· size Large in Green

Instructions in Black apply to both sizes.

GAUGE INFORMATION

In pattern,

2 repeats (12 sts) = 3½" (9 cm);

32 rnds = 4½" (11.5 cm)

TECHNIQUES USED

- K2 tog *(Fig. 4, page 44)*
- SSK *(Figs. 5a-c, page 44)*

Alternate working two rounds of each color, carrying the unused yarn up the back. Slipping a stitch combines two colors that look like you changed colors.

When instructed to slip a stitch, always slip as if to **purl**.

COWL

With 24" (61 cm) circular needle and MC, cast on 102{204} sts **loosely** *(see Using Circular Needles, page 43)*; place a marker to indicate the beginning of the round *(see Markers, page 42)*.

Rnd 1 (Right side)**:** Knit around.

Rnd 2: Purl around; drop MC.

Rnd 3: With CC, ★ K3, wyib slip 1, K1, wyib slip 1; repeat from ★ around.

Rnd 4: ★ K3, wyib slip 1, P1, wyib slip 1; repeat from ★ around; drop CC.

Rnd 5: With MC, knit around.

Rnd 6: Purl around; drop MC.

Rnd 7: With CC, ★ wyib slip 1, K1, wyib slip 1, K3; repeat from ★ around.

Rnd 8: ★ Wyib slip 1, P1, wyib slip 1, K3; repeat from ★ around; drop CC.

Rnd 9: With MC, knit around.

Rnds 10-38: Repeat Rnds 2-9, 3 times; then repeat Rnds 2-6 once **more**.

Cut CC.

With MC, bind off all sts **loosely** in **knit**.

HAT
Ribbing

With 16" (40.5 cm) circular needle and MC, cast on 60{72} sts **loosely**; place a marker to indicate the beginning of the round.

Rnds 1-12: ★ K3, P3; repeat from ★ around.

Body

Rnd 1 (Right side)**:** Knit around.

Rnd 2: Purl around; drop MC.

Rnd 3: With CC, ★ K3, wyib slip 1, K1, wyib slip 1; repeat from ★ around.

Rnd 4: ★ K3, wyib slip 1, P1, wyib slip 1; repeat from ★ around; drop CC.

Rnd 5: With MC, knit around.

Rnd 6: Purl around; drop MC.

Rnd 7: With CC, ★ wyib slip 1, K1, wyib slip 1, K3; repeat from ★ around.

Rnd 8: ★ Wyib slip 1, P1, wyib slip 1, K3; repeat from ★ around; drop CC.

Rnd 9: With MC, knit around.

Rnds 10-22: Repeat Rnds 2-9 once, then repeat Rnds 2-6 once **more**.

Cut CC.

With MC, knit every round until piece measures approximately 7" (18 cm) from cast on edge.

SHAPING

Change to double-pointed needles when there are too few stitches to use a circular needle *(see Using Double-Pointed Needles, page 43).*

Rnd 1: ★ K2 tog, K 11{14}, SSK; repeat from ★ around: 52{64} sts.

Rnd 2: Knit around.

Rnd 3: ★ K2 tog, K9{12}, SSK; repeat from ★ around: 44{56} sts.

Rnd 4: Knit around.

Rnd 5: ★ K2 tog, K7{10}, SSK; repeat from ★ around: 36{48} sts.

Rnd 6: Knit around.

Rnd 7: ★ K2 tog, K5{8}, SSK; repeat from ★ around: 28{40} sts.

Rnd 8: Knit around.

Rnd 9: ★ K2 tog, K3{6}, SSK; repeat from ★ around: 20{32} sts.

Rnd 10: ★ K2 tog, K1{4}, SSK; repeat from ★ around: 12{24} sts.

SIZE LARGE ONLY

Rnd 11: ★ K2 tog, K2, SSK; repeat from ★ around: 16 sts.

BOTH SIZES

Rnd 11{12}: ★ K2 tog, SSK; repeat from ★ around: 6{8} sts.

Cut yarn leaving an 8" (20.5 cm) length for sewing.
Thread yarn needle with end and slip remaining sts onto yarn needle; pull **tightly** to close and secure end.

GENERAL INSTRUCTIONS

ABBREVIATIONS

CC	Contrasting Color
cm	centimeters
K	knit
LPC	Left Purl Cross
LT	Left Twist
M1	Make one
MC	Main Color
mm	millimeters
P	purl
Rnd(s)	round(s)
RPC	Right Purl Cross
SSK	slip, slip, knit
st(s)	stitch(es)
tog	together
wyib	with yarn in back
wyif	with yarn in front
YO	yarn over

SYMBOLS & TERMS

★ — work instructions following ★ as many **more** times as indicated in addition to the first time.

( ) or [ ] — contains explanatory remarks.

colon (:) — the number(s) given after a colon at the end of a round denotes the number of stitches you should have on that round.

GAUGE

Exact gauge is essential for proper size and fit. Before beginning your project, make a sample swatch in the yarn and needles specified in the individual instructions. After completing the swatch, measure it, counting your stitches and rows/rounds carefully. If your swatch is larger or smaller than specified, **make another, changing needle size to get the correct gauge.** Keep trying until you find the size needles that will give you the specified gauge.

KNIT TERMINOLOGY	
UNITED STATES	**INTERNATIONAL**
gauge =	tension
bind off =	cast off
yarn over (YO) =	yarn forward (yfwd) **or** yarn around needle (yrn)

KNITTING NEEDLES																			
U.S.	0	1	2	3	4	5	6	7	8	9	10	10½	11	13	15	17	19	35	50
U.K.	13	12	11	10	9	8	7	6	5	4	3	2	1	00	000	---	---	---	---
Metric - mm	2	2.25	2.75	3.25	3.5	3.75	4	4.5	5	5.5	6	6.5	8	9	10	12.75	15	19	25

◼◻◻◻ **BEGINNER**	Projects for first-time knitters using basic knit and purl stitches. Minimal shaping.
◼◼◻◻ **EASY**	Projects using basic stitches, repetitive stitch patterns, simple color changes, and simple shaping and finishing.
◼◼◼◻ **INTERMEDIATE**	Projects with a variety of stitches, such as basic cables and lace, simple intarsia, double-pointed needles and knitting in the round needle techniques, mid-level shaping and finishing.
◼◼◼◼ **EXPERIENCED**	Projects using advanced techniques and stitches, such as short rows, fair isle, more intricate intarsia, cables, lace patterns, and numerous color changes.

Yarn Weight Symbol & Names	LACE 0	SUPER FINE 1	FINE 2	LIGHT 3	MEDIUM 4	BULKY 5	SUPER BULKY 6	JUMBO 7
Type of Yarns in Category	Fingering, size 10 crochet thread	Sock, Fingering, Baby	Sport, Baby	DK, Light Worsted	Worsted, Afghan, Aran	Chunky, Craft, Rug	Super Bulky, Roving	Jumbo, Roving
Knit Gauge Ranges in Stockinette St to 4" (10 cm)	33-40 sts**	27-32 sts	23-26 sts	21-24 sts	16-20 sts	12-15 sts	7-11 sts	6 sts and fewer
Advised Needle Size Range	000 to 1	1 to 3	3 to 5	5 to 7	7 to 9	9 to 11	11 to 17	17 and larger

* GUIDELINES ONLY: The chart above reflects the most commonly used gauges and needle sizes for specific yarn categories.

** Lace weight yarns are usually knitted on larger needles to create lacy openwork patterns. Accordingly, a gauge range is difficult to determine. Always follow the gauge stated in your pattern.

SIZING

To determine what size Mitts/Mittens to make, measure around the widest part of your hand, usually across the knuckles *(Fig. 1a)*.

To determine what size Hat to make, measure around the crown of your head with a tape measure *(Fig. 1b)*.

As long as the Hat is made from a yarn with elasticity, the fabric will have some give. You want the band to fit snugly, so choose the size closest to your measurement or slightly smaller. You can also adjust the band size by changing the needle size used for it, and therefore adjusting the gauge and the finished measurement.

MARKERS

As a convenience to you, we have used markers to help distinguish the beginning of a pattern or a round. Place markers as instructed. You may use purchased markers or tie a length of contrasting color yarn around the needle. When you reach a marker on each round, slip it from the left needle to the right needle; remove it when no longer needed.

A split-ring marker is placed around the first stitch on the round to indicate the beginning of the round. Move it up at the end of each round.

Fig. 1a

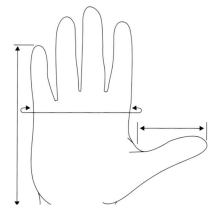

Fig. 1b

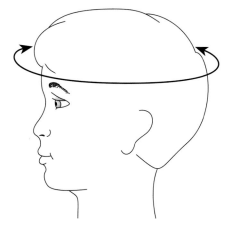

KNITTING IN THE ROUND

Using Circular Needles

When you knit a tube, as for a hat, headband, or cowl, you are going to work around on the outside of the circle, with the **right** side of the knitting facing you.

Using a circular needle, cast on all stitches as instructed. Untwist and straighten the stitches on the needle to be sure that the cast on ridge lies on the inside of the needle and never rolls around the needle.

Hold the needle so that the ball of yarn is attached to the stitch closest to the **right** hand point. Place a marker to mark the beginning of the round.

To begin working in the round, knit the stitches on the left hand point *(Fig. 2)*.

Continue working each round as instructed **without turning the work**; but for the first three rounds or so, check to be sure that the cast on edge has not twisted around the needle. If it has, it is impossible to untwist it. The only way to fix this is to rip it out and return to the cast on round.

Using Double-Pointed Needles

When working a piece that is too small to use a circular needle, double-pointed needles are required. Divide the stitches between three or four double-pointed needles as specified in the individual instructions *(Figs. 3a & b)*. Being careful **not** to twist the cast on ridge, form a triangle or a square with the needles *(Figs. 3c & d)*.

With the working yarn coming from the stitch on the last needle and using the remaining needle *(Fig. 3c)*, work across the stitches on the first needle.

You will now have an empty needle with which to work the stitches from the next needle. Work the first stitch of each needle firmly to prevent gaps. Continue working around without turning the work.

Fig. 3a

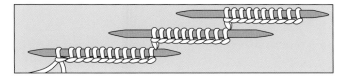

Fig. 3b

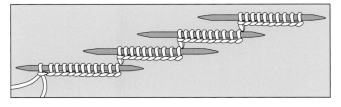

Fig. 2

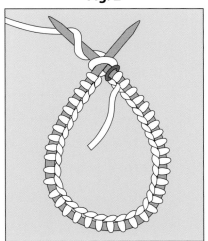

Fig. 3c

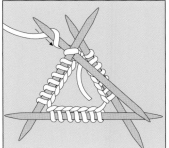

Fig. 3d

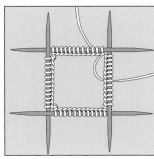

DECREASES

Knit 2 Together
(abbreviated K2 tog)

Insert the right needle into the **front** of the first two stitches on the left needle as if to **knit** *(Fig. 4)*, then **knit** them together as if they were one stitch.

Fig. 4

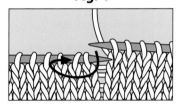

Slip, Slip, Knit
(abbreviated SSK)

Separately slip two stitches as if to **knit** *(Fig. 5a)*. Insert the **left** needle into the **front** of both slipped stitches *(Fig. 5b)* and **knit** them together as if they were one stitch *(Fig. 5c)*.

Fig. 5a

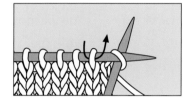

Fig. 5b

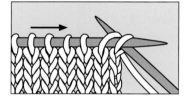

Fig. 5c

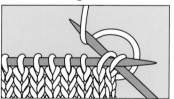

Purl 2 Together
(abbreviated P2 tog)

Insert the right needle into the **front** of the first two stitches on the left needle as if to **purl** *(Fig. 6)*, then **purl** them together as if they were one stitch.

Fig. 6

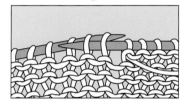

INCREASES

Make One *(abbreviated M1)*

Insert the left needle under the horizontal strand between the stitches from the **front** *(Fig. 7a)*, then **knit** into the back of the strand *(Fig. 7b)*.

Fig. 7a

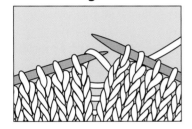

Fig. 7b

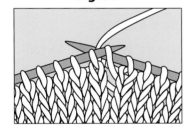

Yarn Over

Bring the yarn forward **between** the needles, then back **over** the top of the right hand needle, so that it is now in position to knit the next stitch *(Fig. 8)*.

Fig. 8

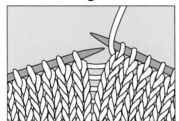

PICKING UP STITCHES

When instructed to pick up stitches, insert the needle from the **front** to the **back** under two strands at the edge of the Gusset *(Fig. 9)*. Put the yarn around the needle as if to **knit**, then bring the needle with the yarn back through the stitch to the right side, resulting in a stitch on the needle.

Fig. 9

YARN INFORMATION

The projects in this book were made using a variety of yarns. Any brand of yarn in the specified weight may be used. It is best to refer to the yardage/meters when determining how many skeins or balls to purchase. Remember, to arrive at the finished size, it is the GAUGE/TENSION that is important, not the brand of yarn.

For your convenience, listed below are the specific yarns and colors used to create our photography models. Because yarn manufacturers make frequent changes in their product lines, you may sometimes find it necessary to use a substitute yarn or to search for the discontinued product at alternate suppliers (locally or online).

DREAMY CABLED
BOOT CUFFS & MITTENS
Red Heart® Dreamy™
#8341 Grey

CLASSIC LACE COWL & HAT
Patons® Classic Wool
DK Superwash™
#12609 Gold

SILKY SATIN HAT
& FINGERLESS MITTS
Bernat® Satin™
#04221 Soft Fern

GO TEAM COWL & HEADBAND
Lion Brand® Hometown USA®
#147 Minneapolis Purple

EASY CABLED
BOOT CUFFS & HEADBAND
Lion Brand® Wool-Ease®
#140 Rose Heather

WRAPPED IN LOVE
COWL & MITTENS
Red Heart® With Love® Metallic
#8524 Teal

CHUNKY SLIPPED STITCH
COWL & HAT
Patons® Shetland Chunky™
MC - #78416 Pretty In Pink
CC - #78008 Aran

JEN LUCAS

Jen has been knitting since 2004 and designing since 2008.
She's designed hundreds of patterns for books, magazines and yarn
companies, in addition to her growing self-published catalog online.
When not knitting or crocheting, you can find Jen reading,
cross stitching, or taking a road trip vacation. She lives in
Fox River Grove, Illinois, with her husband, Alex.

We have made every effort to ensure that these instructions are accurate and complete. We cannot, however, be responsible for human error, typographical mistakes, or variations in individual work.

Production Team: Instructional/Technical Writer - Linda A. Daley; Senior Graphic Artist - Lora Puls; Graphic Artist - Amy L. Teeter; Photo Stylist - Lori Wenger; and Photographer - Jason Masters.

Made in U.S.A.